CUT AND SHUFFLE QUILTS

JAN OCHTERBECK

American Quilter's Society

PO Box 3290 • Paducah, KY 42002-3290
www.AmericanQuilter.com

Located in Paducah, Kentucky, the American Quilter's Society (AQS) is dedicated to promoting the accomplishments of today's quilters. Through its publications and events, AQS strives to honor today's quiltmakers and their work and to inspire future creativity and innovation in quiltmaking.

DIRECTOR OF PUBLICATIONS: KIMBERLY HOLLAND TETREV
SENIOR EDITOR: LINDA BAXTER LASCO
PROOFREADER: ADRIANA FITCH
GRAPHIC DESIGN: CHRIS GILBERT
COVER DESIGN: MICHAEL BUCKINGHAM
PHOTOGRAPHY: CHARLES R. LYNCH

Additional copies of this book may be ordered from the American Quilter's Society, PO Box 3290, Paducah, KY 42002-3290, or online at www.AmericanQuilter.com.

Text and quilt designs © 2015, Author, Jan Ochterbeck
Layout Artwork © 2015, American Quilter's Society

LIBRARY OF CONGRESS CATALOGING-IN-PUBLICATION DATA

Ochterbeck, Jan.
  Cut and shuffle quilts / by Jan Ochterbeck.
    1 online resource.
  Includes bibliographical references and index.
  Description based on print version record and CIP data provided by publisher; resource not viewed.
  ISBN 978-1-60460-304-0 -- ISBN 978-1-60460-209-8 (print)
  1. Patchwork quilts. 2. Patchwork--Patterns. I. Title.
  TT835
  746.46--dc23
                    2015019616

COVER QUILTS: POSITIVITY, detail, full quilt on page 16
LABYRINTH, detail, full quilt on page 52

TITLE PAGE: POSITIVITY, detail, full quilt on page 16

ACKNOWLEDGMENTS

◇◇◇◇◇◇◇◇◇◇◇◇◇◇◇◇◇◇◇◇◇◇

This book would not have been possible without the encouragement of many people—family, friends, and fellow quilters—and I thank them all wholeheartedly. I appreciate the confidence and support of my editors, Elaine Brelsford and Linda Baxter Lasco, in making this project happen. Special thanks go to the following: Sandy Etheridge, Lois Hays, Suzanne Marshall, Darlene Pratte, and Marilyn Raphael.

I also gratefully appreciate the assistance of Nancy Jewell and Westminster Fibers in providing the Kaffe Fassett prints used in HEAT WAVE. And I especially appreciate the encouragement of my husband, Gary, without whose support this book would never have been possible.

■ ■ ■ ■ ■ ▦ ▦ ■ ▦ ■ ▦ ▦ ■ ▦ ■

LEFT: SINGING THE BLUES, detail. Full quilt on page 43.

CONTENTS

◇◇◇◇◇◇◇◇◇◇◇◇◇◇◇◇◇

LEFT: HEAT WAVE, detail. Full quilt on page 34.

INTRODUCTION

◇◇◇◇◇◇◇◇◇◇◇◇◇◇◇◇◇◇

When I was a color specialist for a major US footwear company, one of my duties was to send color standards to our China office so the material sourcing team could match those colors in leather and fabrics. In apparel and accessories product development, a *color standard is the parent color* of all the colored materials that are dyed to match it.

My Chinese colleagues were proficient in English, but the translations of *color standard* and *parent color* were a little awkward for them. They solved the communication problem by calling the color standard the *color mama*. I loved it! They found a very effective shortcut to convey the meaning needed.

The premise of this book is that you can easily make a variety of simple yet versatile quilt blocks by making a parent block, slicing and dicing it, shuffling the parts, and reassembling them Nine-Patch style. Every block starts with the parent block. Let's call it the *Block Mama*, shall we?!

We'll start with the Block Mama and create four different blocks, which we'll then use in six varied quilt designs.

Once you have mastered the Block Mama and the blocks, you can use them to create original quilts of your own. I hope you'll enjoy creating Block Mama quilts as much as I have enjoyed designing them for you.

▪ ▪

LEFT: POSITIVITY, detail. Full quilt on page 16.

ADDITIONAL TECHNIQUES

Making the binding

■ Cut the number of 2½" x WOF strips specified in the pattern.

■ Join end-to-end. Fold in half lengthwise, right sides together, and press. Set aside.

Adding borders

■ Mark the top and bottom borders at the center and the quarters.

■ Mark the top and bottom edges of the quilt top in the same way.

■ Pin the borders to the quilt top at the top and bottom, matching the marks.

■ Sew the borders to the quilt. Press the seams toward the borders.

■ In the same way, mark the sides of the quilt top and the side borders. Pin, then sew to the quilt. Press the seams toward the borders.

Finishing

■ Piece the backing according to the measurements given in the pattern.

■ Layer the quilt with the backing face down, batting, and top face up; baste.

■ Quilt as desired. (Notes on how each of the quilts was quilted are given in the patterns.)

■ Square-up and trim the quilt, trimming ⅛" beyond the edge of the outer border.

■ Sew the binding to the front of quilt, using a scant ⅛" seam allowance.

■ Hand or machine stitch the binding down to the back.

■ Be sure to label your quilt!

The Block Mama

The Block Mama

We'll start with the Block Mama and introduce several variations of shuffled and reconfigured blocks. All the blocks finish at 12" x 12" (12½" x 12½" with seam allowances) *except* the Block Mama, which is 13½" x 13½" to allow for additional cutting and seam allowances.

THE BLOCK MAMA

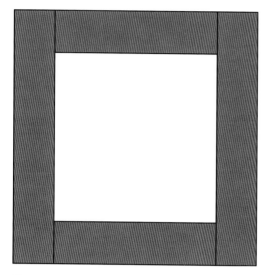

Fig. 1. The Block Mama

Before you begin

Every block featured in *Cut and Shuffle Quilts* starts with this simple framed square (fig. 1).

For one block, you will need a fat quarter (FQ) or ⅓ linear yard of background fabric, and ¼ yard (either FQ or linear) of contrasting accent color. If using pre-cuts, a Layer Cake™ piece can be used for the background, and two of the same print Jelly Roll™ strips can be used for the accent color.

For multiple blocks in the same quilt, total fabric requirements are given in the instructions for the quilts.

Fig. 2. Block Mama cut pieces

Cutting

- Cut 1 – 9½" x 9½" square from the background fabric.

- Accent color: cut strips 2½" wide.

- If you're using a fat quarter of the accent color, cut 3 strips perpendicular to the selvage. If you're using linear yardage, cut 2 width-of-fabric (WOF) strips OR you can use 2 matching Jelly Roll strips. From the accent strips, cut 2 pieces 2½" x 9½" and 2 pieces 2½" x 13½" (fig. 2).

Making the Block Mama (All seams are a scant ¼".)

- Sew a 9½" strip of accent color to the top and bottom of the background square. Press the seams toward the accent color (fig. 3a).

- Sew the 13½" strips of accent color to the left and right sides. Press the seams toward the accent color (fig. 3b).

Fig. 3a. Block Mama assembly   **Fig. 3b.** Completed Block Mama

The Block Mama is now complete and you can use it to create any of the featured blocks on the following pages. The Block Mama should measure 13½" x 13½" square.

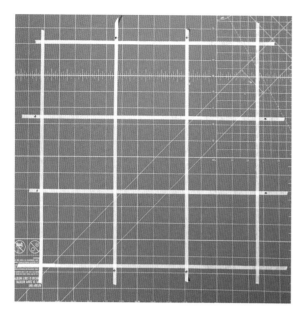

Fig. 4. Mat marked with tape for cutting

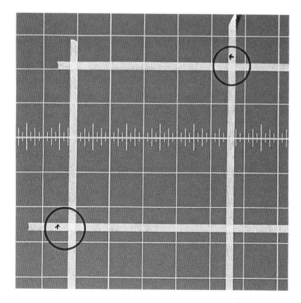

Fig. 5. Tape marked with arrows

Cutting the Block Mama into Pieces

All of the blocks featured in this book require the Block Mama to be cut into nine pieces that are then shuffled and reassembled. It is crucial to cut accurately. To do so, I strongly recommend marking your cutting mat. Mine is shown here marked with ¼" quilter's tape. The total square must be 13½" x 13½" on the inside of the taped lines.

1. Start on the left and lay the tape to the left (outside) of a line on your mat. This is your first vertical tapeline (fig. 4).

2. Starting from the right edge of the tape, measure 4½" over to the right and lay another line of tape next to your ruler. This is your second vertical tapeline (fig. 4).

3. Measure 4½" over to the right again, this time starting from the left edge of the tape. Your third tapeline's left edge will now be 9" from your first tapeline.

4. Repeat. Your fourth tapeline's left edge will be 4½" from your third tapeline. Double-check that the inside measurement between the first and fourth tapelines is 13½."

5. Rotate your cutting mat 90-degrees (one-quarter turn) counterclockwise and repeat, starting with tapeline 5 at the left.

6. Repeat step 2, resulting in tapeline 6.

7. Repeat step 3, resulting in tapeline 7.

8. Repeat step 4, resulting in tapeline 8.

9. Double-check all your measurements.

10. Note with arrows which side of the tapeline to use (fig. 5).

Cutting the Block Mama into Pieces (Continued)

- To cut the Block Mama into pieces, lay it on the cutting mat within the outer marked square and tape it down (fig. 6).
- Cut 4½" away from the left edge and again 4½" away from the first cut, using the tapelines as guides. Measure and cut carefully (fig. 7).
- Rotate the mat one-quarter turn and repeat, cutting in the other direction (fig. 8).
- The cut parts can now be shuffled as needed for the specific block you're making. Refer to the individual block instructions for further directions for each block (fig. 9).

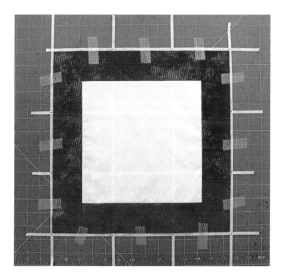

Fig. 6. Block Mama positioned for cutting

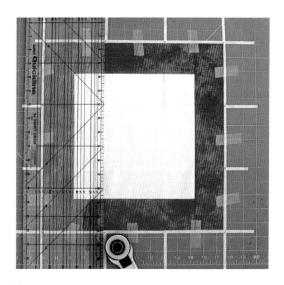

Fig. 7. Cutting the Block Mama

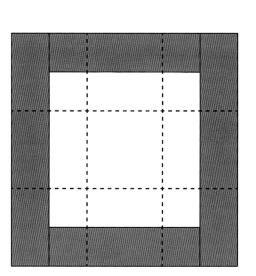

Fig. 8. Cutting lines for the Block Mama

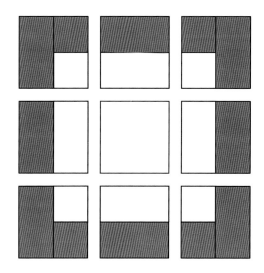

Fig. 9. Cut Block Mama

THE PLUS BLOCK

This block is used in **POSITIVITY** on page 16.

The Plus Block

THE PLUS BLOCK

A NOTE ABOUT FABRIC SELECTION

Avoid directional fabrics for the frame. I recommend fabrics that read solid or near-solid, such as batiks or tone-on-tones.

If using a directional background fabric, instead of rotating the corner units, swap the diagonal corners. The resulting plus shape will be the same, but the directional fabrics will remain aligned correctly.

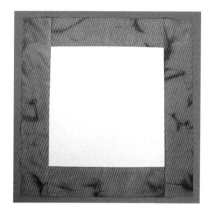

Fig. 1. Block Mama for the Plus Block

Making the Block (All seams are scant a ¼".)

- For each block you will need:
  - ☐ 1 — 9½" x 9½" square of background fabric
  - ☐ 2 — 9½" x 2½" strips of contrasting fabric
  - ☐ 2 — 2½" x 13½" strips of contrasting fabric

- Make the Block Mama (page 9) and cut it into 9 parts (fig. 1).

Fig. 2. Cut parts positioned for the Plus Block

- Rotate the corners inward so that the accent color makes a fat outline around a plus-sign shape of the background fabric, as shown in fig. 2.

- Sew the units into rows.

- Press seams of the top and bottom rows out toward the corners. Press the seams of the middle row toward the center.

- Sew rows together, locking seam allowances and matching the corners (fig. 3).

Fig. 3. Completed Plus Block

- Press seams toward the outside.

POSITIVITY

◇◇◇◇◇◇◇◇◇◇◇◇◇◇◇◇◇◇◇◇◇◇

POSITIVITY, 60" x 60". Made by the author.
Quilted by Darlene Pratte, St Louis, Missouri.

Positivity

60" x 60"

Skill Level: Easy to Intermediate

Uses the **Plus Block** from page 14

Fabric Requirements

- 1⅝ yards background (light pink)

- ¼ yard each of 9 different accent colors, tone-on-tone prints, or batiks (If using only one accent color fabric, 1 yard is sufficient for 9 blocks.)

- 2⅜ yards focus print (includes binding)

- 4 yards backing

- 68" x 68" batting

A NOTE ABOUT FABRIC SELECTION

POSITIVITY works best when a pale solid or light-value, low-volume print is used for the background; a focus print is used for the sashing and borders; and batiks, solids, or prints that read solid are used for the accent colors in the blocks.

Prints can also be used for the accent colors in the blocks if there is strong value contrast between the print, the background, and the sashing fabric.

Cutting

Background (light pink)

- Cut 9 – 9½" x 9½" squares.

- Cut 5 – 4½" x WOF strips.
    - ☐ Subcut 12 – 4½" x 12½" pieces.
    - ☐ Subcut 4 – 4½" x 4½" squares.
    - ☐ Subcut 24 – 2½" x 4½" pieces.

Accent colors, each

- If using linear yardage, cut 2 – 2½" x WOF strips (18 total) OR if using fat quarters, cut 3 – 2½" strips perpendicular to the selvage (27 total).

    - ☐ Subcut 2 – 2½" x 13½" pieces (18 total) and 2 – 2½" x 9½" pieces (18 total).

Focus Print, used for sashing, border, and binding

- Cut 4 – 4½" x WOF strips; subcut 64 – 2½" x 4½" pieces.

- Cut 1 – 2½" x WOF strip; subcut 16 – 2½" x 2½" squares.

- Cut 6 – 4½" x WOF strips for borders (*trimmed to size later*).

- Cut 7 – 2½" x WOF strips for the binding.

Block Assembly

Follow the detailed instructions for the Plus block (page 14), make 9 blocks, 1 with each accent fabric (fig. 1).

Top Assembly with Sashing

- Arrange the blocks on a design wall and determine color placement, following the top assembly diagram (page 20) .

- To make the sashing strips, add a 2½" x 4½" focus fabric piece to each end of a 2½" x 4½" background fabric piece. Make 24 sashing units. Press the seams toward the focus fabric (fig. 2).

- Add a 2½" x 2½" print cornerstone to one end of 12 sashing strips. Add a cornerstone to the other end of 4 of them. Press the seams away from the cornerstones (fig. 3a and fig. 3b).

- Join one sashing strip to the right-hand side of each block. Add a sashing strip to the left-hand side of the blocks in your left column. Press the seams toward the sashing (fig. 4a and fig. 4b).

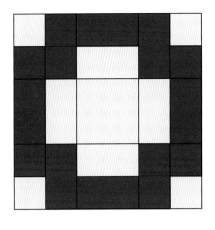

Fig. 1

Fig. 2

Fig. 3a

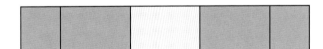

Fig. 3b

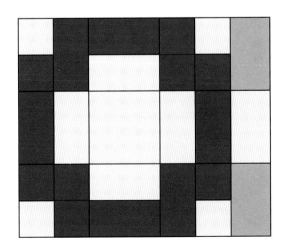

Fig. 4a

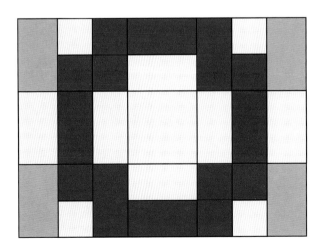

Fig. 4b

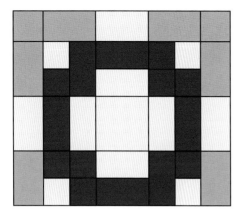

Fig. 5a

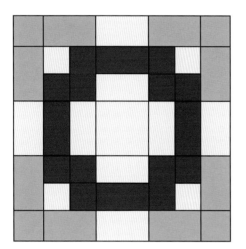

Fig. 5b

Top Assembly with Sashing (Continued)

■ Add the sashing units to the tops of all the blocks and to the bottoms of the 3 blocks that will be on your bottom row. Press the seams toward the sashing (fig. 5a and fig. 5b).

■ Join the blocks into rows. Press seams of the top and bottom rows to the left and seams of the middle row to the right.

■ Join the rows together (fig. 6).

Fig. 6. Top Assembly

Borders

First Border

- Sew 2½" x 4½" focus print pieces to one end of each 4½" x 12½" background piece, and to the other end of 4 of them. Join them into strips as shown in fig. 7. Press the seams toward the focus print sashing. Make 4. These borders should measure 44½" long.

Fig. 7

- Sew 4½" x 4½" squares of background (light pink) to the ends of 2 of the borders. Press the seams toward the focus print sashing. These borders should measure 52½" long (fig. 8).

Fig. 8

- Sew the 44½" borders to the top and bottom of the quilt center, matching the sashing seams. Press the seams toward the border.
- Sew the 52½" borders to the sides of the quilt center, matching the sashing seams. Press the seams toward the border (fig. 9).

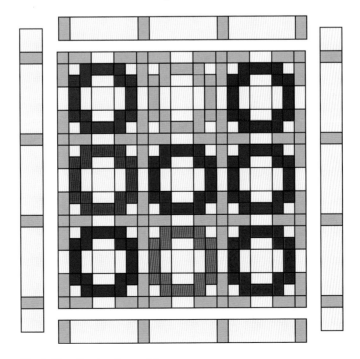

Fig. 9. First Border Assembly

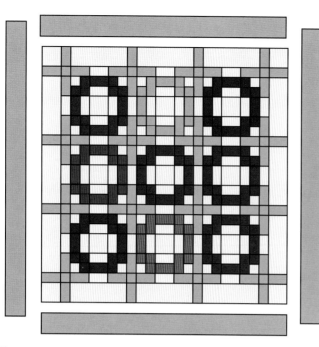

Fig. 10. Second Border Assembly

Fig. 11

Outer Border

Piece outer borders

- Trim 4 of the 4½" x WOF focus print strips to measure 40½" long.

- From the remaining 4½" x WOF strips, cut 2 – 12½" pieces and 2 – 20½" pieces.

- Sew the 12½" pieces to 2 of the 40½" strips, resulting in 52½" strips. Add to the top and bottom of the quilt center. Press the seams toward the border.

- Sew the 20½" pieces to 2 of the 40½" strips, resulting in 60½" strips. Add to the sides of the quilt center. Press the seams toward the border (figs. 10 and 11).

Finishing

- **Backing:** Piece the backing to measure at least 68" x 68".

- POSITIVITY was longarm quilted using an allover pantograph.

- Refer to the finishing instructions (page 8) to complete your quilt.

Alternate Colorway Suggestions for POSITIVITY

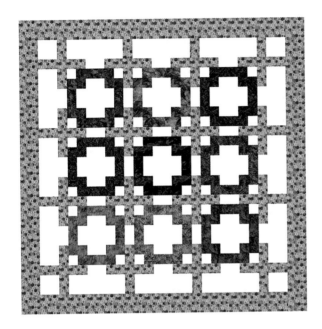

Illustrated using Izumi, Bali Batiks, and Bali Handprints by Hoffman California International Fabrics®

Illustrated using Give Thanks by Deb Strain for Moda and Bali Batiks by Hoffman California International Fabrics®

Illustrated using Washi by Rashida Coleman-Hale for Timeless Treasures

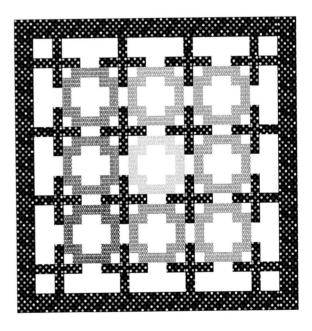

Illustrated using Basic Brights black dot by Windham Fabrics and Pezzi Prints by American Jane for Moda

THE FOUR CORNERS BLOCK

This block is used in **SCOOT,** on page 28, and in **HEAT WAVE** on page 34.

Four Corners Version a

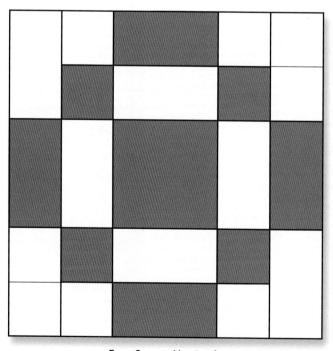

Four Corners Version b

THE FOUR CORNERS BLOCK

Versions A and B

The Four Corners block works well in settings where positive and negative versions of the block are used. Version A (fig. 1) uses the quilt's background fabric for the center of the Block Mama and an accent fabric for the frame. Version B (fig. 2) uses an accent fabric for the center of the Block Mama and the background fabric for the frame.

SCOOT (page 28) uses both Version A and Version B, with a printed background fabric and solid accent colors. HEAT WAVE (page 34) uses version A with a dark background fabric and various accent prints for the frames.

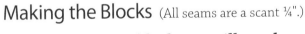

Making the Blocks (All seams are a scant ¼".)

For the Version A block you will need

- 1 – 9½" x 9½" square of background fabric
- 2 – 2½" x 9½" strips of the accent fabric
- 2 – 2½" x 13½" strips of the accent fabric
- Make the Block Mama (page 9) and cut it into 9 parts (fig. 3).

For the Version B block you will need

- 1 – 9½" x 9½" square of the accent fabric
- 2 – 2½" x 9½" strips of background fabric
- 2 – 2½" x 13½" strips of background fabric

Fig. 1. Four Corners, Version a: Block Mama with background fabric center and accent fabric frame

Fig. 2. Four Corners, Version b: Block Mama with accent fabric center and background fabric frame

Fig. 3. Version a. Cut parts positioned for the Four Corners block

Fig. 4. Version b. Cut parts positioned for the Four Corners block

Fig. 5. Version a. Completed Four Corners block

Fig. 6. Version b. Completed Four Corners block

Making the blocks (Continued)

■ Make the Block Mama and cut it into 9 parts.

For both versions, only the middle units are moved. Within each block, swap the middle top and bottom units and the middle left and right units (figs. 3 and 4).

■ Sew the parts into rows (figs. 5 and 6). Press as directed for the specific quilt you are making. If no specific pressing instructions are given, press as follows:

  ☐ **Version A:** Press seams of the top and bottom row in toward the center. Press the seams of the middle row out toward the sides.

  ☐ **Version B:** Press the seams of the top and bottom row out toward the corners. Press seams of the middle row toward the center.

■ Sew rows together, locking seam allowances and matching corners. Press as noted for the specific quilt you are making. If no specific pressing instructions are given, press as follows:

  ☐ **Version A:** Press row seams toward the outside.

  ☐ **Version B:** Press row seams toward the center.

A NOTE ABOUT DIRECTIONAL FABRIC:

The examples shown in the Four Corners block assembly photographs use a directional fabric with a horizontal pattern for the accent fabric.

In Version A, if using a directional fabric, decide if it must all go the same direction or if it's okay for some to go vertical and some to go horizontal. In this example, the pattern is going in both directions. I recommend mixing it up, to give you flexibility to rotate blocks later if needed for better seam allowance management.

If you prefer the pattern to go all in one direction, cut your 2½" x 13½" strips on the lengthwise grain of the fabric (parallel to the selvage) instead of using WOF strips. Cut your 2½" x 9½" strips on the crosswise grain.

In Version B, because you start with a large print square, your pattern will end up going all in the same direction. If you want to mix it up, rotate the cut center unit one-quarter turn.

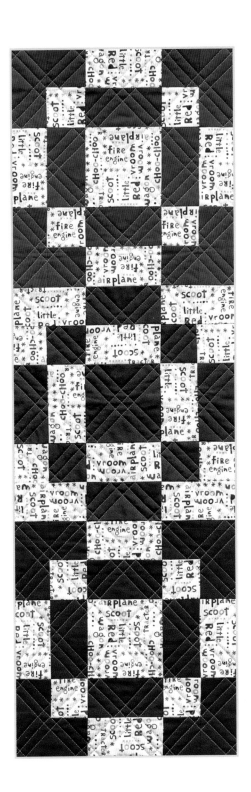

SCOOT

SCOOT, 40" x 40". Made and quilted the author. Fabrics from the author's stash including the Scoot collection by Deena Rutter for Riley Blake Designs and Kona® Cotton by Robert Kaufman Fabrics.

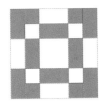

Scoot

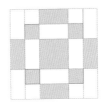

60" x 60"

Skill Level: Easy

Uses the **Four Corners Block** from page 24

Fabric Requirements

- 1⅜ yards print background
- ¼ yard blue
- ¼ yard red
- ⅜ yard OR a fat quarter of medium green
- ⅜ yard OR a fat quarter of dark green
- ½ yard binding
- 1¾ yards backing
- 48" x 48" batting

A NOTE ABOUT FABRIC SELECTION:

The Four Corners layout used for Scoot works best with strong value contrast. A light-value, low-volume print or solid is recommended for the background, and high-contrast solids or prints are suggested for the blocks.

This small quilt size is ideal for baby quilts using pale juvenile prints, combined with coordinating solids or tone-on-tones.

Cutting

Background (SCOOT Print)

- Cut 1 – 9½" WOF strip; subcut 4 – 9½" x 9½" squares.

- Cut 1 – 12½" x WOF strip; subcut 1 – 12½" x 12½" square.

- From the remainder of the 12½" WOF strip, cut 3 – 2½" strips on the cross grain.
  - Subcut 2 of the strips into 4 – 2½" x 9½" pieces for the blocks.
  - Subcut 1 strip 2½" x 13½" for the blocks.

- Cut 1 – 2½" x WOF strip; subcut 3 – 2½" x 13½" pieces for the blocks.

- Cut 4 – 2½" x WOF strips for the borders; trim away the selvages.
  - Trim 2 strips to measure 36½" long.
  - Trim 2 strips to measure 40½" long.

Accent colors

- **Red:** Cut 3 – 2½" x WOF strips OR, if using fat quarters, cut 6 – 2½" strips.
  - Subcut 4 – 2½" x 9½" pieces.
  - Subcut 4 – 2½" x 13½" pieces.

- **Blue:** Cut 3 – WOF strips OR, if using fat quarters, cut 6 – 2½" strips.
  - Subcut 4 – 2½" x 9½" pieces.
  - Subcut 4 – 2½" x 13½" pieces.

- **Medium green:** Cut 2 – 9½" x 9½" squares.

- **Dark green:** Cut 2 – 9½" x 9½" squares.

Binding

- Cut 5 strips 2½" x WOF.

Fig. 1

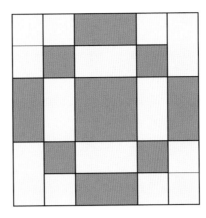

Fig. 2

Fig. 3

Block Assembly

- Follow the detailed instructions for the Four Corners block (page 24).

- Make 2 Version A blocks with red trim and 2 Version A blocks with blue trim (fig. 1).

- Make 2 Version B blocks with medium green centers and 2 Version B blocks with dark green centers (fig. 2).

Top Assembly

- Join blocks and the plain 12½" x 12½" square into rows. *Note:* If you rotate alternate blocks (in this case the green ones) one-quarter turn, you will have fewer seams to match when joining the rows together (fig. 3).

- Arrange the blocks according to the top assembly diagram (fig. 4).

- Press the seams of the top and bottom rows toward the outside blocks; press the seams of the middle row toward the center block.

- Sew the rows together. Press the seams toward the center.

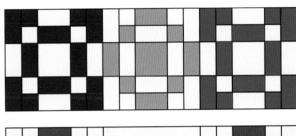

Fig. 4. Top Assembly

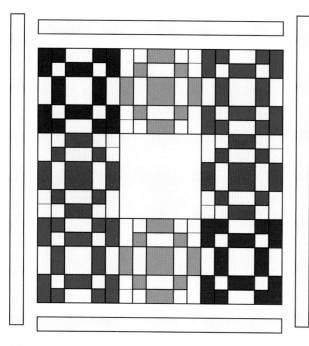

Fig 5a. Border Assembly

Borders

- Add the 36½" border strips to the top and bottom of the quilt center (page 8).

- Add the 40½" border strips to the sides (figs. 5a and b).

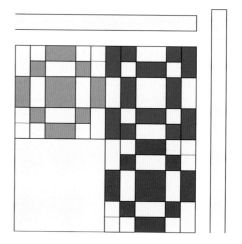

Fig 5b. Border Assembly (enlarged)

Finishing

- Piece the backing to measure at least 44" x 44".

- SCOOT was quilted in a straight-line, triple diagonal grid using a walking foot.

- Refer to the finishing instructions (page 8) to complete your quilt (fig. 6).

Fig. 6

Alternate Colorway Suggestions for SCOOT

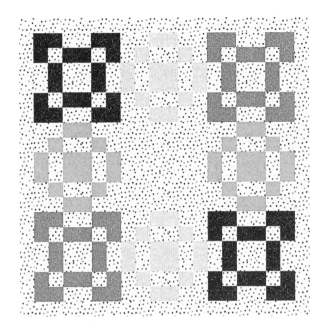

Illustrated using Bungle Jungle by Tim and Beck for Moda

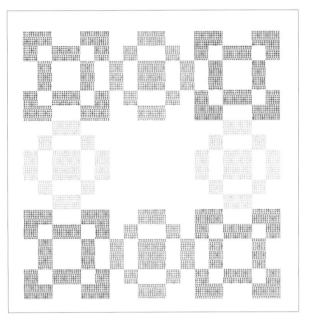

Illustrated using Squared Elements by AG Studio for Art Gallery Fabrics, (with white)

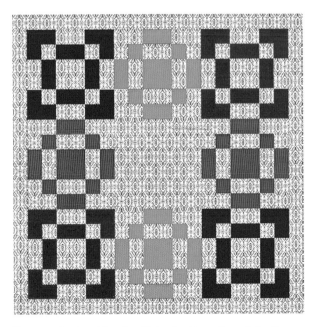

Illustrated using Morning Tides by Marc Cesarik for Free Spirit (with solids)

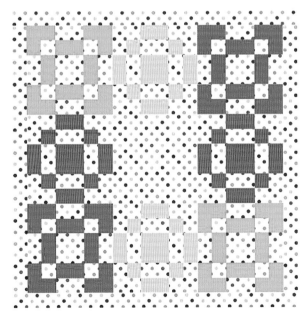

Illustrated using Spintastic by Laura Beringer for Marcus Fabrics®

HEAT WAVE

HEAT WAVE, 58" x 72". Made by the author. Quilted by Darlene Pratte, St Louis, Missouri. Kaffe Fassett prints courtesy of Westminster Fibers

HEAT WAVE

58" x 72"

Skill Level: Easy to Intermediate

Uses the **Four Corners Block** from page 24

Fabric Requirements

- 2½ yards black crosshatch print (includes binding)

- ¼ yard OR a fat quarter each of 20 Kaffe Fassett prints for the blocks (See the note below.)

- 1 yard purple dot print for sashing

- ½ yard yellow print for the sashing

- 4¾ yards for the backing

- 66" x 80" batting

A NOTE ABOUT FABRIC SELECTION:

Twelve different Kaffe Fassett prints were chosen for the twenty blocks in this quilt. Ten to twenty different prints can be used, making one or two blocks from each print. Two blocks can be cut from ⅜ yard of fabric.

The palette should be all warm colors. Any combination of medium-value Kaffe Fassett prints in pink, red, orange, brown, and gold will work; avoid very dark or very pale prints. A darker print that harmonizes, such as the purple dot used in the sample, should be used for the sashing, highlighted with a bright yellow print, which should be the lightest print in this quilt.

To balance and complement the bright colors and provide contrast, an off-black crosshatch is used in the sample. Solid jet black would be too harsh. The subtle print features charcoal crosshatching on a black background. For simplicity in the instructions below, this is referred to as black.

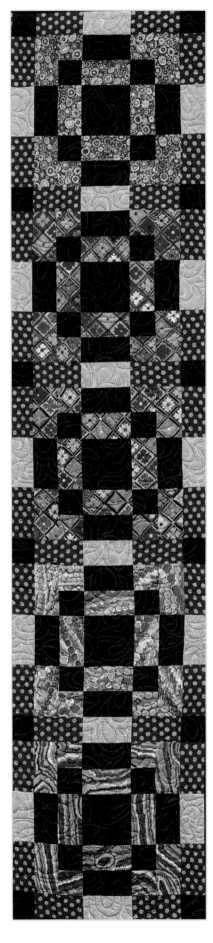

Cutting

Black crosshatch

- Cut 5 – 9½" x WOF strips
  - ☐ Subcut 20 – 9½" x 9½" squares for the Block Mamas.

- Cut 2 – 2½" x WOF strips
  - ☐ Subcut 30 – 2½" x 2½" squares for the cornerstones.

- Cut 8 – 2½" x WOF strips for the binding.

Prints for Blocks if using 20 different prints

- If using WOF yardage, cut 2 – 2½" wide strips of each print.
  - ☐ Subcut 2 – 2½" x 13½" pieces and 2 – 2½" x 9½" pieces.

- If using fat quarters, cut 1 strip perpendicular to the selvage
  - ☐ Subcut 2 – 2½" x 9½" pieces. Then cut 2 – 2½" strips parallel to the selvage
  - ☐ Subcut 2 – 2½" x 13½" pieces.

Prints for Blocks if using 10 different prints

- If using WOF yardage, cut 3 – 2½" wide strips.
  - ☐ Subcut 4 – 2½" x 13½" pieces.
  - ☐ Subcut 4 – 2½" x 9½" pieces.

- If using fat quarters, cut 6 – 2½" strips perpendicular to the selvage
  - ☐ Subcut 4 – 2½" x 9½" pieces from 2 of the strips
  - ☐ Subcut 4 – 2½" x 13½" pieces from the remaining strips.

Purple Dot for the Sashing

- Cut 7 – 4½" x WOF strips; subcut 98 – 2½" x 4½" pieces.

Yellow Print for Sashing

- Cut 3 – 4½" WOF strips, then subcut 49 – 2½" x 4½" pieces.

Block Assembly

Following the detailed instructions for the
Four Corners block (page 24), make 20 blocks of
version A, using black for the background (fig. 1).

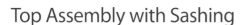

Top Assembly with Sashing

- Lay out blocks on design wall and determine
color/print placement.

- To make the sashing strips, join a 2½" x 4½"
purple dot piece to each end of a 2½" x 4½"
yellow print piece (fig. 2). Make 49 units.
Press the seams of 25 sashing units toward
the yellow center; press the seams of the
remainder toward the purple dot.

- Using the sashing strips with the seams
pressed toward the purple dot fabric, join
one sashing strip to the top of each block (fig.
3). Press the seams toward the block. Add a
sashing strip to the bottom of the blocks in
your bottom row. Press the seams toward the
block.

- Add a 2½" black cornerstone to one end of
each of the remaining sashing strips (fig. 4a).
Add a cornerstone to the other end of 5 of
them (fig. 4b).

- Press the seams toward the cornerstones.

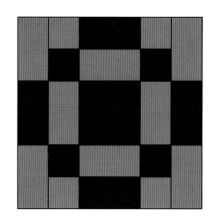

Fig. 1

Fig. 2

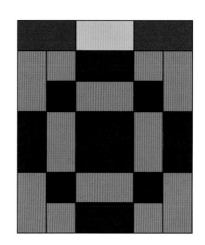

Fig. 3

Fig. 4a

Fig. 4b

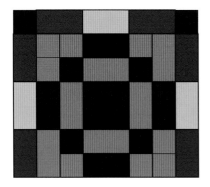

Fig. 5a

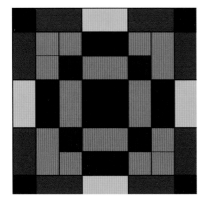

Fig. 5b

Top Assembly with Sashing (Continued)

■ Add the sashing units to the left of all blocks and to the right of the blocks that will be on your right column (fig. 5a). Do not press the seams yet.

■ Add the sashing units to the top of all blocks and to the bottom of the blocks that will be on your bottom row (fig 5b).

■ Join the blocks into rows (fig. 6). Press the seams of rows 1, 3, and 5 to the left. Press the seams of rows 2 and 4 to the right.

■ Join the rows together (fig. 7). Press all the seams in one direction.

Finishing

■ Piece the backing to measure at least 70" x 84".

■ HEAT WAVE was longarm quilted using an allover pantograph.

■ Refer to the finishing instructions (page 8) to complete your quilt.

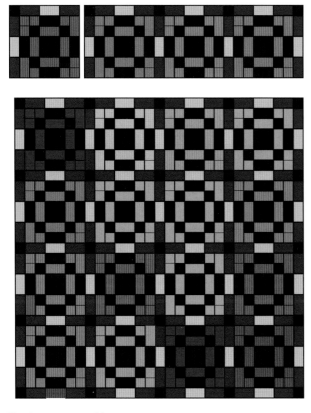

Fig. 6. Top Assembly

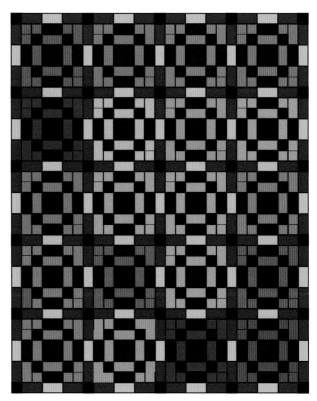

Fig. 7

Alternate Colorway Suggestions for HEAT WAVE

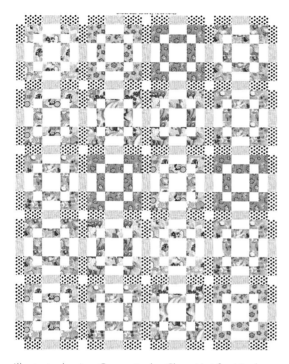

Illustrated using Coquette by Chez Moi for Moda

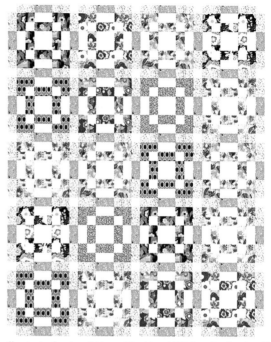

Illustrated using Urban Mod by AGF Studio for Art Gallery Fabrics

Illustrated using Urbanista by Michael Miller Fabrics

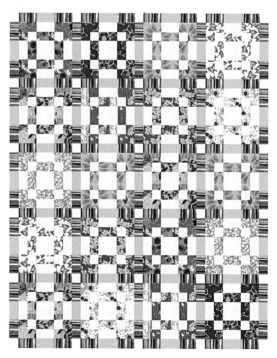

Illustrated using Sleeping Beauty by Nel Whatmore for Free Spirit

THE ALTERNATE FOUR CORNERS BLOCK

These blocks are used in SINGING THE BLUES on page 43.

Alternate Four Corners Block, Medium Frame

Alternate Four Corners Block, Dark Frame

THE ALTERNATE FOUR CORNERS BLOCK

Two Block Mamas using the same background fabric for the centers create the Alternate Four Corners blocks. After the Block Mamas are cut, the Alternate Four Corners blocks are formed when the top, bottom, and side units are rotated and swapped between the two blocks.

Making the Blocks (All seams are scant a ¼".)

- For each pair of blocks you will need:
  - ☐ 2 – 9½" x 9½" squares of background fabric, shown here as the palest print
  - ☐ 2 – 2½" x 9½" strips and 2 – 2½" x 13½" strips of medium fabric
  - ☐ 2 – 2½" x 9½" strips and 2 – 2½" x 13½" strips of dark fabric

Fig. 1a. Block Mama for Alternate Four Corners block: Dark Frame

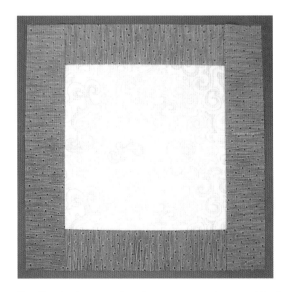

Fig. 1b. Block Mama for Alternate Four Corners block: Medium Frame

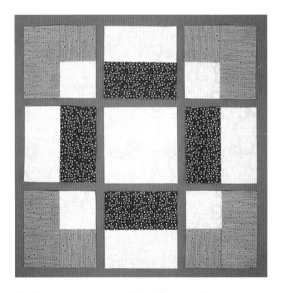

Fig. 2a. Parts positioned for Alternate Four Corners block: Medium Frame

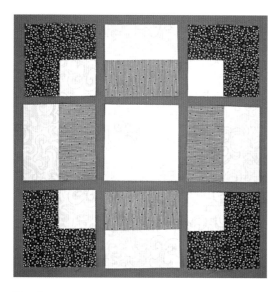

Fig. 2b. Parts positioned for Alternate Four Corners block: Dark Frame

Making the blocks (Continued)

- Make a Block Mama (page 9) in each colorway (figs. 1a and 1b) and cut both into 9 parts.

- Swap the top, bottom, and side units between the blocks, and rotate them so the frame color is inward (figs. 2a and fig. 2b).

- Sew the units into rows. Press the seams in the top and bottom rows inward; press the seams in the middle row outward.

- Sew the rows together, locking the seam allowances and matching the corners (figs. 3a and 3b). Press the row seams toward the outside.

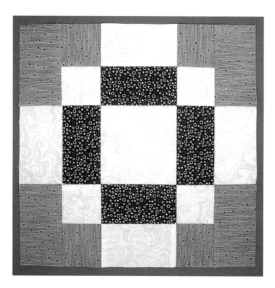

Fig. 4a. Completed Alternate Four Corners block: Medium Frame

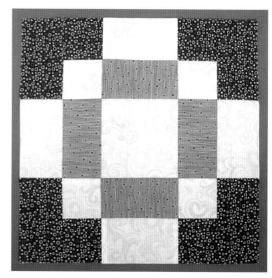

Fig. 4b. Completed Alternate Four Corners block: Dark Frame

A Note About Fabric Selection

For best results, choose fabrics with strong value contrast between the background and the frame colors and between the two shades used for the frames.

Singing the Blues

✕✕✕✕✕✕✕✕✕✕✕✕✕✕✕

Singing the Blues, 64" x 76". Made by the author. Quilted by Darlene Pratte, St Louis, Missouri. Fabrics from the author's stash including Symphony in Blue collection from Connecting Threads

SINGING THE BLUES

64" x 76" With optional border as shown

60" x 72" Without border

Skill Level: Easy

Uses the **Alternate Four Corners Block** from page 40

Fabric Requirements

- 3 yards pale background print (2½ yards without border)
- 1½ yards dark blue print
- 1½ yards medium blue print
- ¾ yard binding (same dark blue print as used in the blocks)
- 5 yards backing
- 72" x 84" batting (68" x 80" without optional border)

Optional Border

When there are a lot of seams at the edge of a quilt, I sometimes add a small border to help hold it all together. I've used a 2" wide border of the background fabric on SINGING THE BLUES, but for a more modern effect you can choose to omit the border.

Without the border, the quilt is still a nice throw size, 60" x 72". Fabric requirements are given for both with and without the border.

Cutting

Pale Background

- Cut 8 – 9½" WOF strips
  - ☐ Subcut 30 – 9½" x 9½" squares.

Dark blue print and medium blue print EACH

- Cut 10 – 2½" x WOF strips
  - ☐ Subcut 3 – 2½" x 13½" pieces per strip for a total of 30 – 2½" x 13½" pieces of each color.

- Cut 8 – 2½" x WOF strips
  - ☐ Subcut 4 – 2½" x 9½" pieces per strip for a total of 30 – 2½" x 9½" pieces of each color.

Pale background for the optional border

- Cut 7 – 2½" x WOF strips.

- Piece as needed to cut 2 border strips 2½" x 60½" and 2 border strips 2½" x 76½".

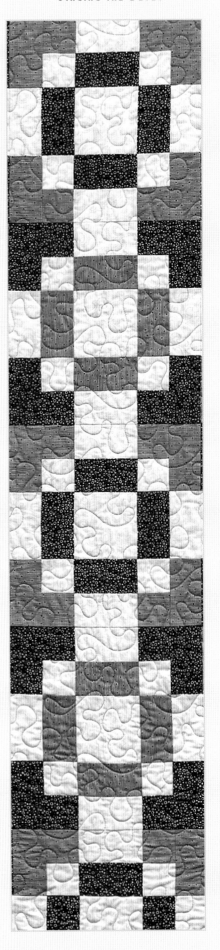

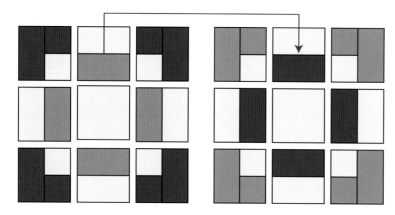

Fig. 1a

Block Assembly

Following the detailed instructions for the Alternate Four Corners blocks (page 40), make 15 Block Mamas with dark blue frames and 15 Block Mamas with medium blue frames (figs. 1a and 1b).

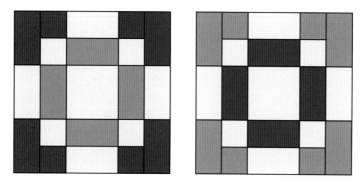

Fig. 1b

Top Assembly

Fig. 2. Partial Top Assembly

- Arrange the blocks, alternating medium and dark color placement, according to the top assembly diagram (fig. 2).

- Join the blocks into rows. To minimize matching seams and to lock seam allowances together, rotate alternate blocks one-quarter turn (fig. 3).

- Press the seams of the odd rows to the left and the even rows to the right.

- Sew the rows together. Press all the seams in one direction.

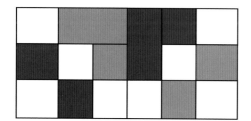

Fig. 3

Optional Border

- Add the 60½" border strips to the top and bottom and the 76½" border strips to the sides (figs. 4a and 4b).

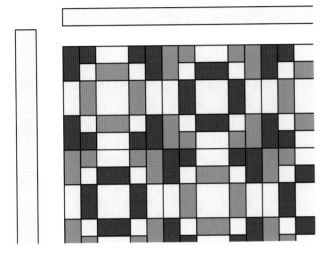

Fig. 4a. Border Assembly (enlarged)

Fig. 4b. Border Assembly

Finishing

- Piece the backing to measure at least 70" x 82".

- SINGING THE BLUES was allover longarm quilted.

- Refer to the finishing instructions (page 8) to complete your quilt.

Fig. 5

Alternate Colorway Suggestions for SINGING THE BLUES

Illustrated using Quilt of Valor colors

Illustrated using Amelia by Jo Morton for Andover Fabrics™

Illustrated using Good Seasons Summer by Carol Eldridge for Andover Fabrics™
(Using print for background fabric)

Illustrated using Downton Abbey by Kathy Hall for Andover Fabrics™

THE LABYRINTH BLOCK

This block is used in LABYRINTH, on page 52 and in ZEN GARDEN, on page 57.

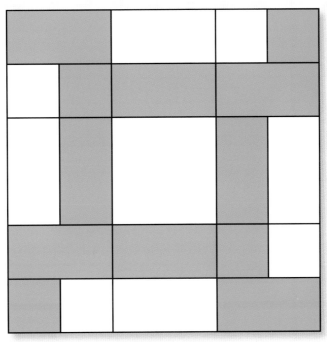

Labyrinth Block, Version a

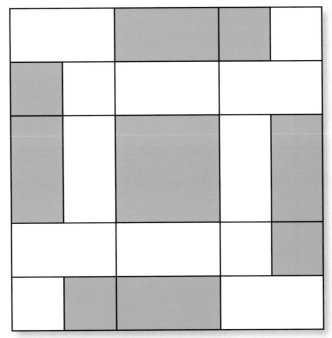

Labyrinth Block, Version b

THE LABYRINTH BLOCK

Fig. 1. Labyrinth Block, Version a: Block Mama

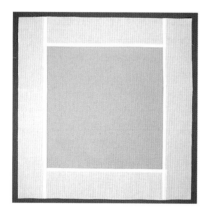

Fig. 2. Labyrinth Block, Version b: Block Mama

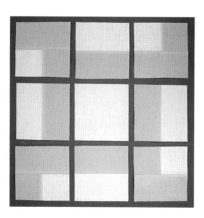

Fig. 3. Parts positioned for Labyrinth Block: Version a

Versions A and B

The Labyrinth block works well in settings where positive and negative versions of the block are used.

Version A uses the quilt's background fabric for the center of the Block Mama and an accent color for the frame (fig. 1). Version B uses the accent color for the center of the Block Mama and the background fabric for the frame (fig. 2).

LABYRINTH (page 52) uses both Versions A and B. ZEN GARDEN (page 57) uses only Version A. Both result in maze-like layouts.

Making the Block (All seams are scant a ¼".)

For the Version A block you will need

- ☐ 1 – 9½" x 9½" square of background fabric
- ☐ 2 – 2½" x 9½" strips of an accent color fabric
- ☐ 2 – 2½" x 13½" strips of an accent color fabric

■ Make the Block Mama (page 9) and cut it into 9 parts.

For the Version B block you will need

- ☐ 1 – 9½" x 9½" square of the accent fabric
- ☐ 2 – 2½" x 9½" strips of background fabric
- ☐ 2 – 2½" x 13½" strips of background fabric

■ Make the Block Mama (page 9)and cut it into 9 parts.

- Within each block, rotate the top middle, bottom middle, and side units a half turn (or swap the top and bottom units and left and right units).

- Rotate the corner units a quarter turn clockwise (figs. 3 and 4).

- Sew the parts into rows (figs. 5 and 6). *Note:* there will be seams where the seam allowances do not lock together; pin carefully to prevent mismatched seams.

- **Version A:** Press the seams of the top and bottom rows toward the center. Press the seams of the middle row toward the sides.

- **Version B:** Press the seams of the top and bottom rows towards the corners. Press the seams of the middle row toward the center.

- Sew rows together, locking seam allowances where possible and matching corners. Again, there will be seams where the seam allowances do not lock together; pin carefully to prevent mismatched seams.

- **Pressing:** This will help ensure that seam allowances lock together as much as possible when assembling quilt top.

- **Version A:** Press the row seams toward the outside.

- **Version B:** Press the row seams toward the center.

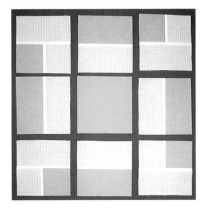

Fig. 4. Parts positioned for Labyrinth Block: Version b

Fig. 5. Completed Labyrinth Block: Version a

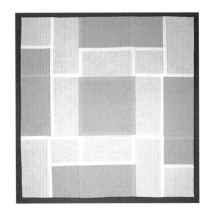

Fig. 6. Completed Labyrinth Block: Version b

A NOTE ABOUT FABRIC SELECTION:

Strong value contrast is required to achieve the maze-like effect. Solids, or fabrics that read as solid, work best. A very even, small-scale, allover print can work if paired with a strongly contrasting solid.

LABYRINTH

LABYRINTH, 60" x 72". Made and quilted by the author. Fabrics from the author's collection: Kona® Cotton in Azure and Snow from Robert Kaufman Fabrics

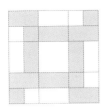

LABYRINTH

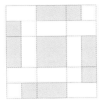

60" x 72"

Skill Level: Easy to Intermediate

Uses the **Labyrinth Block** from page 49

Fabric Requirements

- 3¼ yards aqua (includes ¾ yard binding)

- 2½ yards white

- 4 yards backing

- 68" x 80" batting

A NOTE ABOUT FABRIC SELECTION:

Due to the busyness of the piecing, LABYRINTH works best in fabrics that read solid, such as Stonehenge, some batiks, some tone-on-tones, and very small-scale allover prints. The fabrics used should contrast strongly with each other in value. A patterned print could work as long as it's small in scale and it's used with a strongly contrasting solid.

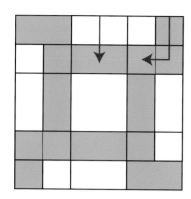

Fig. 1

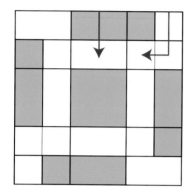

Fig. 2

Cutting

From BOTH aqua and white:

- Cut 4 – 9½" x WOF strips
  - Subcut 15 – 9½" x 9½" squares (total 30).

- Cut 8 – 2½" x WOF strips
  - Subcut 4 – 2½" x 9½" pieces per strip for a total of 30 – 2½" x 9½" pieces (total 60).

- Cut 10 – 2½" x WOF strips
  - Subcut 3 – 2½" x 13½" pieces per strip for a total of 30 pieces (total 60).

- Cut 8 – 2½" strips of aqua for binding.

Block Assembly

Following the detailed instructions for the Labyrinth block (page 49), make 30 blocks—15 Version A with white centers and 15 Version B with aqua centers (figs. 1 and 2).

Fig. 3. Top Assembly

Top Assembly

- Join blocks into rows, alternating Version A and B as shown in fig. 3, Top Assembly. For best interlocking of nine patch seam allowances, rotate alternate blocks one quarter turn.

- Press seams of odd rows to the left and even rows to the right.

- Sew rows together (fig. 4).

- Press seams open, or press all in one direction.

Finishing

- Piece the backing to measure at least 68" x 80".

- Layer backing face down, batting, and top face up; baste.

- LABYRINTH was quilted by the author in concentric arcs using the walking foot.

- Refer to the finishing instructions (page 8) to complete your quilt.

Fig. 4

Alternate Colorway Suggestions for LABYRINTH

Illustrated using Kona® Cotton by Robert Kaufman Fabrics in Coral and Bone

Illustrated using Stonehenge by Northcott Fabrics

Illustrated using April in Paris (text print) by Timeless Treasures with Kona® Cotton in Ash

Illustrated using Island Batiks by Robert Kaufman Fabrics

ZEN GARDEN

ZEN GARDEN, 76" x 88". Made by the author. Quilted by Sandy Etheridge, St Louis, Missouri. Fabrics from the author's stash including Plume by Timeless Treasures and La Scala by Robert Kaufman Fabrics

 ZEN GARDEN

76" x 88"

Skill Level: Easy to Intermediate

Uses the **Labyrinth Block** from page 49

Fabric Requirements

- 3½ yards navy (includes ¾ yard for binding)
- 2½ yards white-on-white
- ¾ yard inner border
- 2¾ yards outer border
- 8 yards backing
- 84" x 96" batting

Cutting

White-on-White Backgroud

- Cut 8 – 9½" x WOF strips.
  - ☐ Subcut 30 – 9½"x 9½" squares.

Navy

- Cut 20 – 2½" x WOF strips for the blocks
  - ☐ Subcut 3 – 2½" x 13½" pieces per strip for a total of 60 – 2½" x 13½" pieces.

- Cut 15 – 2½" x WOF strips for the blocks
  - ☐ Subcut 4 – 2½" x 9½" by pieces per strip for a total of 60 – 2½" x 9½" pieces.

Inner Border

- Cut 7 – 2½" x WOF strips.

Outer Border

- Cut 2 lengthwise (parallel to the selvage) strips 6½" wide x length of fabric (trimmed to length later).

- Cut 6 – 6½" strips crosswise from the remainder of the fabric

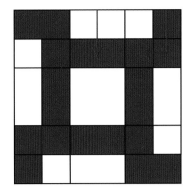

Fig. 1

Block Assembly

Following the detailed instructions for the Labyrinth block (page 49), make 30 Version A blocks (fig. 1).

Top Assembly

- Arrange the blocks according to the top assembly diagram (fig. 2).

- Join the blocks into rows. For best interlocking of the seam allowances, rotate alternate blocks one-quarter turn.

- Press the seams of the odd rows to the left and even rows to the right OR press the seams open. Trim the navy where any seam allowances are pressed toward the white to prevent show-through.

- Sew the rows together. Press the seams open OR press them all in one direction. Trim the navy where any seam allowances are pressed toward the white.

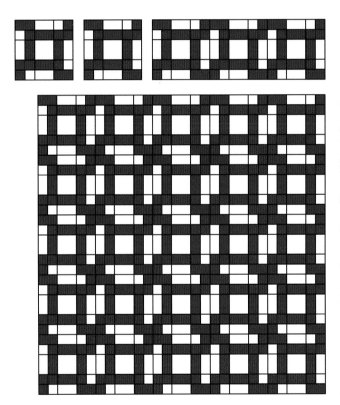

Fig. 2. Top Assembly

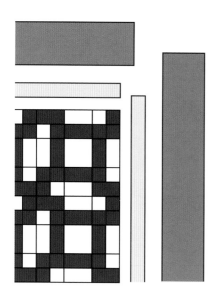

Fig. 3a. Border Assembly (enlarged)

Borders

Inner Border

- Piece the inner border strips as needed and cut 2 – 2½" x 60½" strips. Add to the top and bottom (figs. 3a and 3b). Press the seams toward the borders.

- Cut 2 – 2½" x 76½" strips. Add to the sides (figs. 3a and 3b). Press the seams toward the borders.

Outer Border

- Piece the outer border strips as needed and cut 2 – 6½" x 64½" strips. Add to the quilt top and bottom (fig. 4). Press the seams toward the borders.

- Trim 2 of the strips cut on the lengthwise grain to 6½" x 88½". Add to the sides (fig. 4). Press the seams toward the borders.

Fig. 3b. Border Assembly

Finishing

- Piece the backing to measure at least 86" x 98".

- ZEN GARDEN was custom longarm quilted with pebbles in the white areas and water in the navy area.

- Refer to the finishing instructions (page 8) to complete your quilt.

Fig. 4. Top Assembly

Alternate Colorway Suggestions for ZEN GARDEN

Illustrated using Acacia by Tula Pink for Free Spirit

Illustrated using Felicity by Bren Talavera for Robert Kaufman Fabrics

Illustrated using Nouveau Rouge by Alice Kennedy for Timeless Treasures

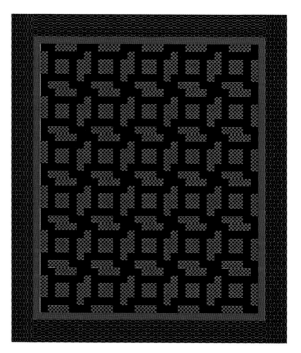

Illustrated using Mod Guys and Uptown Urban by Michael Miller Fabrics

About the Author

Jan Ochterbeck has been interested in fabric and sewing all her life. Like many quilters today, she started making doll clothes as a very young child. From age eight her ambition was to become a fashion designer. She attended Stephens College in Columbia, Missouri, where she graduated with a bachelor of fine arts degree in fashion design.

Jan worked professionally in apparel, textiles, and footwear product development for over 35 years. Her jobs have included pattern making, designing apparel, color and trend research, technical color approval, and color and material library management.

A quilter since the early 1990s, Jan is mostly self-taught, drawing on her sewing and professional experience to figure out patterns and piecing. Now retired, Jan is focusing on her quilting career as a new chapter in her life. She designs patterns, blogs at TheColorfulFabriholic.blogspot.com, lectures, and teaches.

Jan lives in the St. Louis, Missouri area with her husband. She has one son and one grandson. Besides quilting, Jan's interests are reading, blogging, and traveling, especially to her favorite beach on the Gulf Coast.

Jan Ochterbeck

#1650

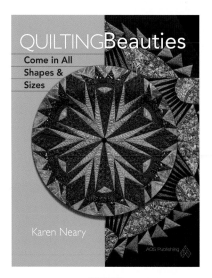

#1647

#8663

▪▫▪ More AQS Books ▪▫▪

This is only a small selection of the books available from the American Quilter's Society. AQS books are known worldwide for timely topics, clear writing, beautiful color photos, and accurate illustrations and patterns. The following books are available from your local bookseller, quilt shop, or public library.

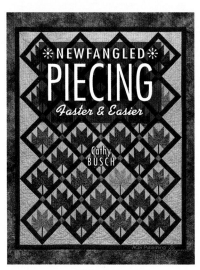

#1420

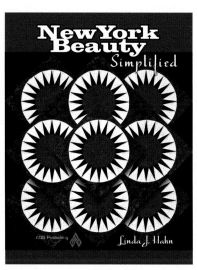

#8346

#8662